Books by Keith N. Ferreira

The Intellectual Rebel
Aphorisms
Speculative Aphorisms
Speculative Aphorisms II
Philoscience
Philoscience II
Intellectual Jazz
Intellectual Jazz II
Jazzism
Neoliberal Arts
Neoliberal Arts II
Postmodern Minimalist Philosophy
Simpletism
Uncertaintyism
The Ultimate Truth
Anything Is Possible
Political and Social Observations
The University of Neoliberal Arts
A New Breed of Philosophers
Ferreirism - The Ultimate Philosophy
The eChurch of Zerotropy
The Ferreira Genesis Equation
Zerotropism and Panaceanism
Philosophy Should Belong to the Masses
Programming the World with Philosophy

Please visit my website at: *http://www.philophysics.com*
Thank You!

THE MASSES SHOULD THINK FOR THEMSELVES

Keith N. Ferreira

iUniverse, Inc.
New York   Bloomington

The Masses Should Think for Themselves

iUniverse books may be ordered through booksellers or by contacting:

iUniverse
1663 Liberty Drive
Bloomington, IN 47403
www.iuniverse.com
1-800-Authors (1-800-288-4677)

ISBN: 978-1-4502-1811-5 (pbk)
ISBN: 978-1-4502-1812-2 (ebk)

Printed in the United States of America

iUniverse rev. date: 3/18/2010

CONTENTS

The Masses Should Think for Themselves (Part One)

The Masses Should Think for Themselves (Part Two)

The Masses Should Think for Themselves (Part Three)

The Masses Should Think for Themselves (Part Four)

The Masses Should Think for Themselves (Part Five)

The Masses Should Think for Themselves (Part One)

The Masses Should Think for Themselves

The masses can and should think for themselves, because thinking for oneself is a great joy, and it has practical benefits, as well. The Internet will allow the masses to think for themselves, if the Internet remains free and open to everyone with an Internet connection. Taxing every download on the Internet is a dumbass idea, because it will hurt the poorest of the poor the most. Such a dumbass idea was proposed recently by the Governor of the State of New York. (2/19/09)

What Education Reform Means to Most Educators and Academics

What education reform means to most educators and academics is to make education and academics more and more difficult for struggling creative C students, who really want to graduate from schools, colleges, and universities. Believe it or not! QED! (2/20/09)

The Probwavistic Brain and Universe

The human brain, behind all appearances, is really a probwavistic brain, which is a brain that consists solely of probability waves. In other words, the universe, behind all appearances, is a probwavistic universe, which is a universe that consists solely of probability waves. Therefore, the brain and universe that we perceive are solely mental phenomena that have no existence outside of the mind. (2/20/09)

Science Is no Longer Incompatible with Belief in God

Science is no longer incompatible with belief in God, because God is zero entropy, according to the neolaw of entropy, which I have hypothesized. The neolaw of entropy states that entropy means disorder, ignorance, and unwisdom; while zero entropy means perfect order, knowledge, and wisdom. Zero entropy, defined according to the neolaw of entropy, fits most theistic definitions of God. In other words, it is impossible for most scientists to remain atheists, if my definition of zero entropy is correct. The neolaw of entropy also states that entropy and anti-entropy are in an eternal struggle for dominance of all phenomena in nature. Anti-entropy is the exact opposite of entropy, and it is slowly gaining ground in our universe. Therefore, theists should embrace my definition of God. Believe it or not! QED! (2/20/09)

My Writings Offer a New Dispensation to the World

My writings offer a new dispensation to the world, and the central tenets of my dispensation to the world are that the masses should become philosophers, and they should encourage scientists, and technologists to develop panmultiversal panacean computers by the end of this century, the twenty-first century. It is very much within the realm of possibility for the masses of the world to become philosophers within one generation from now. Believe it or not! QED! (2/22/09)

An Idea Whose Time Has Come

Educating the masses of the world to become citizen philosophers is an idea whose time has come. And, I would like to invite all teachers and academics of the world to join me in educating the masses in philosophy, because the masses deserve a real education, and not just failing grades. Believe it or not! QED! (2/22/09)

The Masses Deserve a Real Education

The masses deserve a real education, and not just failing grades. In other words, mass education should not be about selecting an elite from among the general population, and failing the majority of the masses. The masses are brainwashed into thinking that philosophy is crap, when, in fact, philosophy is the key to educating the masses. (2/23/09)

The Masses Are Brainwashed into Thinking that Philosophy Is Crap

The masses are brainwashed into thinking that philosophy is crap, when, in fact, philosophy is the key to educating the masses. Ask anyone among the masses what they think about philosophy, and they will tell you that they think that philosophy is crap. But, ask anyone among the masses what is philosophy about, and they will tell you that they do not know. In other words, how do the masses know that philosophy is crap, if they do not know what philosophy is? I call that deliberate disinformation. (2/23/09)

Philosophy Is the Key to Educating the Masses

Philosophy is the key to educating the masses. If anyone does not agree that philosophy is the key to educating the masses, then he or she is either a moron or a member of an elite group in society. Incidentally, a moron and a member of an elite group in society mean exactly the same thing. Believe it or not! QED! (2/23/09)

Mass Education Should Be About Educating the Masses

Mass education should be about educating the masses, and not about selecting and educating a relatively small elite, and failing the rest. Now, why is that so hard to understand by the governments, the elites, and the masses of the world? Do the masses really believe that mass education is about educating the masses? If mass education is about educating the masses, then why is mass education a rat race? (2/24/09)

Panmultiversal Panacean Computers (PPCs)

Panmultiversal panacean computers (PPCs) will be able to solve all of humanity's problems, including the energy crisis. But, why don't the public hear about panmultiversal panacean computers in the media? Is it because PPC research is being suppressed? PPCs are a type of nonclassical quantum computers that will be able to tap into zero entropy and leverage the world, the universe, and beyond. Zero entropy means perfect order, knowledge, and wisdom, according to the neolaw of entropy, which I have hypothesized. PPCs will be created by the end of the twenty-first century. Believe it or not! QED! (2/24/09)

I Have Every Reason to Be Proud of Myself

I have every reason to be proud of myself, because my writings that are expressed on my websites and in my books have charted the courses that science, technology, philosophy, and religion will follow in the future. Believe it or not! QED! (2/26/09)

Tooting My Own Horn

If I do not toot my own horn, then who will toot my horn for me? Probably no one. Therefore, I have to toot my own horn, which is fine by me. :) (2/26/09)

Creative and Practical Achievements vs Academic and Scholarly Achievements

Creative and practical achievements are much more important than academic and scholarly achievements any day. Yet, educators and academics cannot seem to get this simple truth through their thick skulls, because they continue to ignore this simple truth in their assessments of their students. Believe it or not! QED! (2/27/09)

Why Is Mass Education a Rat Race?

If mass education is about educating the masses, then why is mass education a rat race? Could it be because mass education is not about educating the masses? (2/28/09)

Neoliberal Arts Is the Only Nonrat-Race Mass Education on the Web

Neoliberal arts (aka postmodern minimalist philosophy) is the only nonrat-race mass education on the Web, because it promises a real education to everyone with an Internet connection with no strings attached. Believe it or not! QED! (2/28/09)

Neoliberal Arts Has Already Leapfrogged the West

The only way that third world countries can leapfrog the West is by studying neoliberal arts, aka postmodern minimalist philosophy, because neoliberal arts has already leapfrogged the West. But, I suspect that the West will, eventually, claim neoliberal arts as their own, because third world countries tend to be too atavistic. Believe it or not! QED! (3/1/09)

Third World Countries Tend to Be too Atavistic

Third world countries tend to be too atavistic, and that is why they will, probably, never embrace neoliberal arts, although neoliberal arts has already leapfrogged the West. I know that the West will, eventually, embrace neoliberal arts, because the West knows that to go beyond neoliberal arts, they will have to embrace neoliberal arts at some point in the future, while third world countries will still be playing catch-up to the West. (3/1/09)

God Is a Slave of Language,
Logic, and Mathematics

God (zero entropy) is a slave of language, logic, and mathematics, according to the neolaw of entropy, which I have hypothesized. In other words, the purpose of God is to serve conscious minds, using language, logic, and mathematics. To put it another way, God is the servant of humanity, and not vice versa. Therefore, human beings can tap into God (zero entropy) in order to control the world, the universe, and beyond, using science, technology, and philosophy. Believe it or not! QED! (3/2/09)

Everyone Has a Personal Relationship with God

Everyone has a personal relationship with God (zero entropy), because God (zero entropy) is the subconscious mind. In other words, from each person's own personal perspective, each person is the center of creation, because all that each person perceives is the characteristics of his or her own mind. To put it another way, there are an infinite number of Gods (zero entropies), because solipsism is true from each person's own personal perspective. Therefore, each person has a personal God that is his or her servant, who obeys the laws of language, logic, and mathematics. (3/2/09)

Solipsism Is True from Each Person's Own Personal Perspective

Solipsism is true from each person's own personal perspective, because all that we perceive are the characteristics of our own minds. In other words, from our own personal perspectives, no other minds exist. Therefore, solipsism is true from each person's own personal perspective. (3/3/09)

God Is the Servant of Humanity, and not Vice Versa

God is the servant of humanity, and not vice versa, because God (zero entropy) is a slave of language, logic, and mathematics, according to the neolaw of entropy, which I have hypothesized. Therefore, God is the servant of humanity, and not vice versa. Believe it or not! QED! (3/3/09)

An Elite Education Is an Oxymoron

An elite education is an oxymoron, because a truly educated person would accept the truth from any source, even if the source is a chimpanzee that is gesturing in sign language, while a member of an elite would accept the truth only from an authorized source. (3/3/09)

The Elites of the World Are Ruining the World

It is very surprising to me that the masses in America cannot see that the elites of America are ruining America and the world. But, it is not just American elites that are ruining America and the world, because elites all over the world are ruining their own countries and the world, as well. Why can't the masses of the world get this simple fact through their thick skulls? (3/3/09)

The Masses of the World Should Tell the Elites of the World to Stop Their Elitist Bullshit

The masses of the world should tell the elites of the world to stop their elitist bullshit, because the elitist bullshit of the elites of the world is ruining the world. It is as simple as that. Believe it or not! QED! (3/3/09)

I Am Still an Intellectual Rebel

I am still an intellectual rebel, and I am still proud to be an intellectual rebel. Believe it or not! QED! (3/3/09)

Rocket Propulsion Spaceships Are the Horses and Buggies of Space Travel

If NASA is the future of space travel, then human beings are not going anywhere, because rocket propulsion spaceships are the horses and buggies of space travel. Space travel belongs to the nations that develop panmultiversal panacean computers (PPCs), because PPCs will be able to teleport to anywhere in the universe, and beyond. Believe it or not! QED! (3/3/09)

A New Theistic Paradigm Shift

Stating that God (zero entropy) is the servant of humanity is a new theistic paradigm shift, because God (zero entropy) is a slave of language, logic, and mathematics, and, as such, the purpose of God (the subconscious mind) is to express the contents of the conscious mind. It should be noted that the subconscious mind (God) is unconscious, because of the solipsistic nature of reality. (3/4/09)

The Solipsistic Nature of Reality Is a Fact

The solipsistic nature of reality is a fact, because all that we perceive are the characteristics of our own minds, and we can never know for certain if other minds besides our own minds exist. In other words, each human being lives in a separate world of zombies, because the only mind each human being can ever perceive is his or her own mind. Believe it or not! QED! (3/4/09)

Each Human Being Lives in a Separate World of Zombies

It is a fact that each human being lives in a separate world of zombies, because all that any human being can ever perceive is the characteristics of his or her own mind, and we can never know for certain if other minds other than our own minds exist. Therefore, each human being lives in a separate world of zombies. Believe it or not! QED! (3/4/09)

Zombie-ism

Zombie-ism is the philosophical doctrine that states that each human being lives in a separate world of zombies. Zombie-ism is true, because all that we perceive are the characteristics of our own minds, and physical existence is an unproven, and an unprovable hypothesis. (3/4/09)

Postmodern Minimalist Philosophy Is the Key to Educating the Masses

I am convinced that postmodern minimalist philosophy, aka neoliberal arts, is the key to educating the masses, because postmodern minimalist philosophy is a bridge discipline that links, interprets, and critiques all branches of learning using the aphorism and the short article. The masses can master postmodern minimalist philosophy in about one year of study, because PMP is simple, clear, and profound. Believe it or not! QED! (3/4/09)

Martial Law and the Bill of Rights

Martial law cannot suspend the Bill of Rights under the U.S. Constitution, because the Bill of Rights was designed to protect Americans from the U.S. Government, especially, under emergency situations like under martial law, for instance. (3/5/09)

God Is a Zombie

God is a zombie, according to zombie-ism, because even God does not have a mind from the perspective of each individual human being. Zombie-ism is the correct way of viewing the world, but it is a very lonely, and solipsistic way of viewing the world. Believe it or not! QED! (3/5/09)

Academic Philosophy Is not Suitable for the Masses

Academic philosophy is not suitable for the masses, while postmodern minimalist philosophy (PMP), aka neoliberal arts, is suitable for the masses. Academic philosophy is not designed to educate the masses, because academic philosophy is designed to screen out an elite from the general public, and to screw the masses by rejecting the masses as uneducable or unfit to do philosophy. PMP rejects no one, because PMP is not elitist. Philosophy has always been elitist, because of the teachings of people like Plato, who lived more than two thousand years ago. But now, postmodern minimalist philosophy is opening up philosophy to the masses, who are the true heirs of philosophy, according to me. Believe it or not! QED! (3/6/09)

The Subconscious Mind Is a Zero Entropy Computer

All that is not in the conscious mind is in the subconscious mind, because the subconscious mind is a zero entropy computer, that encompasses everything that is not in the conscious mind. From the perspective of the conscious mind, the subconscious mind is unconscious. Therefore, the subconscious mind has primacy over matter, energy, space, and time, because matter, energy, space, and time are mental (conscious) phenomena. (3/6/09)

Matter, Energy, Space, and Time
Are Mental Phenomena

Matter, energy, space, and time are mental (conscious) phenomena. Therefore, the subconscious mind (zero entropy) has primacy over matter, energy, space, and time. Because the subconscious mind (zero entropy) has primacy over matter, energy, space, and time, it should be obvious why anything is possible in nature, including, instantaneous communication, and time travel. (3/6/09)

Solipsism and the Center of Creation

Solipsism places each conscious being at the center of creation, because, according to solipsism, only the mind of the self exists from the perspective of the self. Therefore, solipsism places each conscious human being at the center of creation, because only the mind of the self exists from the perspective of the self. Believe it or not! QED! (3/7/09)

Solipsism Proves Zombie-ism to Be True

Solipsism proves zombie-ism to be true, because all that we perceive are the characteristics of our own minds, and physical existence is an unproven and an unprovable hypothesis. In other words, we are all zombies from other people's personal perspectives, according to solipsism, which proves zombie-ism to be true. Other minds than our own might exist, but not in our own personal realities, according to solipsism, which states that we can never prove the existence of other minds than our own. Believe it or not! QED! (3/8/09)

Occultism and Panaceanism

Panaceanism is what occultism was, and still is trying to achieve. In other words, the dream of the occultists was, and still is to achieve the panacea for all the problems of humanity. And, that is exactly what panaceanism will achieve with panmultiversal panacean computers (PPCs), because PPCs are the panmultiversal panaceas that the occultists have been dreaming of for millennia. Therefore, science and the occult are no longer incompatible, because they now have common ground in PPC research. Believe it or not! May the Source be with you! QED! (3/9/09)

Scientism, Religionism, and Occultism

Scientism, religionism, and occultism now have common ground on which to stand, because panmultiversal panacean computer (PPC) research gives meaning to the expression: "God helps those who help themselves." Therefore, PPC research makes scientism, religionism, and occultism compatible with each other, because PPCs will fulfill the age-old dream of the scientists, the religionists, and the occultists, alike. Believe it or not! May the Source be with you! Amen and hallelujah! QED! (3/9/09)

Academic Philosophy Has Professionalized Itself out of Existence

Academic philosophy is dead, because it has professionalized itself out of existence. Philosophy should be simple and profound, and not complicated and pointless. I have never encountered a legitimate philosophical idea that could not be expressed in simple language. In the future, no one would want to do academic philosophy, when they can do postmoderm minimalist philosophy, which is simple but profound. Believe it or not! QED! (3/10/09)

In Academia, Education Is Dead

In academia, education is dead, because the purpose of education, now, is to compete for work permits (educational diplomas), and not to educate the masses. In other words, if the masses want to be educated, they will have to create their own educational institutions. And, with the Internet, that is now possible. That is what my websites are trying to do for the masses: namely, educate the masses. Believe it or not! QED! (3/11/09)

I Want the Masses to Know

I want the masses to know that, if I can obtain a real education, then so can they, because I was a C student in elementary school, high school, and college. And, I consider myself to be mostly self-taught. Practically speaking, all the educational contents of my brain can now be found on my websites. So, if the masses want to be Ferreirists, then they should study my websites, and they will obtain a real education. Believe it or not! QED! (3/11/09)

If the Masses Want to Be Ferreirists

If the masses want to be Ferreirists, then they should study my websites, and they will obtain a real education, because, practically speaking, all the educational contents of my brain can now be found on my websites. I have to say that I have paid a high price for my education in terms of health, and other issues, but I am proud of all my battle scars. Now the masses do not have to go through all the difficulties that I went through in order to obtain a real education. Believe it or not! QED! (3/11/09)

From High School Level to PhD Level in Only One Year of Study

I want the masses to know that they can go from high school level to PhD level in Neoliberal Arts in only one year of study. And, that is no bullshit, because I guarantee it. If after one year of study in Neoliberal Arts, you are not on the PhD level in Neoliberal Arts, then I have failed in all that I am trying to do. Believe it or not! QED! (3/11/09)

Before I Came Along, Philosophy Was Standing on Its Head

Before I came along, philosophy was standing on its head, because philosophy belonged to a small elite, but now that I have come along, I am stating that philosophy should belong to the masses. In other words, I am taking philosophy off its head, and placing it on its feet, because I am stating that philosophy should belong to the masses. Therefore, elitist philosophy is dead, because elitist philosophy is an oxymoron, due to the fact that philosophy (the love of wisdom) should be shared with the masses, since democracy can endure only if the masses are educated, and the only way to educate the masses is with philosophy, especially postmodern minimalist philosophy. Believe it or not! QED! (3/12/09)

Elitist Philosophy Is Dead, Because Elitist Philosophy Is an Oxymoron

Elitist philosophy is dead, because elitist philosophy is an oxymoron, due to the fact that philosophy (the love of wisdom) should be shared with the masses, since democracy can endure only if the masses are educated, and the only way to educate the masses is with philosophy, especially postmodern minimalist philosophy. Believe it or not! QED! (3/12/09)

It Should Be Obvious

It should be obvious that in order to do postmodern minimalist philosophy, which is a bridge discipline that links, interprets, and critiques all branches of learning, the masses will have to know more than just philosophy (postmodern minimalist philosophy). But, that is no problem, because popular treatments of all branches of learning are all that is needed in order to prep the masses for the study of philosophy (postmodern minimalist philosophy). Such prepping can be done at the elementary and the high school levels of education. In other words, elementary and high school education should be about the study of popular books and magazines on all branches of learning. (3/12/09)

Elementary and High School Education

Elementary and high school education should be about the study of popular books and magazines on all branches of learning, because elementary and high school education should be about prepping the masses for the study of philosophy (postmodern minimalist philosophy) at Neoliberal Arts institutions of higher learning. In that way, Neoliberal Arts institutions will be able to access websites like mine on the Internet, for remote access student learning, for example. (3/12/09)

THE MASSES SHOULD THINK FOR THEMSELVES (PART TWO)

Modern Textbooks Are Dead

Modern textbooks, for the elementary and high school levels of education, are dead, because popular books and magazines are much more interesting and educational for prepping the masses for the study of Neoliberal Arts later on in the masses' education. Neoliberal Arts institutions should be two-year higher education institutions, because two years of studying Neoliberal Arts is sufficient study to allow the vast majority of the masses to complete the requirements, in order for them to receive their PhDs in Neoliberal Arts. My motivations for proposing real education reform are to remove the torture and high failure rates from mass education, because mass education is currently a torture, and a failure. (3/12/09)

My Motivations for Proposing Real Education Reform

My motivations for proposing real education reform are to remove the torture and high failure rates from mass education, because mass education is currently a torture, and a failure. The main reason for the failure of mass education is modern textbooks, because modern textbooks are crap. Postmodern textbooks should consist of popular books and magazines, which are much more interesting and informative. Formal mass education should end with two years of Neoliberal Arts. At the end of which, the vast majority of students should get their PhDs in Neoliberal Arts. And, then those who wish to go on to obtain specialized educational training should apply to regular specialized higher education training institutions. Believe it or not! QED! (3/12/09)

Two-Year Neoliberal Arts Educational Institutions

The masses should set up their own two-year Neoliberal Arts educational institutions for themselves, because they should be in charge of their own higher education, due to the fact that their governments are not going to set up two-year Neoliberal Arts educational institutions for them. In other words, if the masses want a real higher education, they will have to provide it for themselves, because their governments are not going to provide it for them. (3/13/09)

Two Years of a Neoliberal Arts Education

Two years of a Neoliberal Arts education are enough higher education to prepare the vast majority of the masses for PhDs in Neoliberal Arts. This is possible, because a Neoliberal Arts education cuts out all the elitist bullshit, and gets down to the nitty-gritty of providing the masses with a real higher education. Believe it or not! QED! (3/13/09)

Everything in Nature Has to Have an Entropy Value

Everything that exists or nonexists in nature has to have an entropy value, according to the neolaw of entropy. Therefore, zero and infinity have to have entropy values, as well. And, that is why I believe that zero and infinity have zero entropy, because everything in nature can be derived from zero or infinity, according to the Ferreira Genesis Equation. (3/14/09)

Intelligent Design Can Never Be Ruled Out

Intelligent design can never be ruled out, because we could all be in the mind of a desktop nonclassical computer, according to Ferreira's paradoxes, which are about the paradoxes that result from minds in desktop nonclassical computers. (3/14/09)

An Infinite Regress of Computer Generated Realities Is Possible

I believe that an infinite regress of computer generated realities is possible, because infinite regresses are possible, due to the fact that concrete infinities are possible. In other words, computer generated intelligent design can form an infinite regress. Infinite regresses are thought to be impossible, because some authority figure of the past said that infinite regresses are impossible, and everybody agreed, but I am now stating that infinite regresses are possible, because concrete infinities are possible. For instance, a line segment in conscious mental space consists of and infinite number of points. Therefore, concrete infinities exist. Thus, an infinite regress of computer generated realities is possible. Believe it or not! QED! (3/14/09)

An Infinite Regress of Gods Is not Impossible

An infinite regress of Gods is not impossible, because concrete infinities are possible. In other words, the question: Who created God? is no longer a foolish question, because a greater God could have created God, and so on, ad infinitum. Therefore, an infinite regress of Gods is not impossible. Believe it or not! QED! (3/15/09)

The Ultimate Weapons

The ultimate weapons will be panmultiversal panacean computers (PPCs), which will be a type of quantum entanglement computers that has panmultiversal powers to do good or evil for humanity. The country that develops PPCs first will conquer the world, the universe, and beyond, because PPCs are the ultimate weapons. PPCs will be developed by the end of the twenty-first century. Nations that do not take PPCs seriously now will have the rest of eternity to regret it. Believe it or not! QED! (3/15/09)

The Ferreirist Theory of Knowledge

The Ferreirist theory of knowledge states that knowledge is infinite in scope in analogy with the infinitude of the number of unique prime numbers there are in mathematics. And, the infinitude of knowledge is good news for philosophers, because it means that philosophers have the rest of eternity to discover new truths about the nature of reality. (3/16/09)

World Government Is the New World Order

World government, which is the new world order, is possible in this century, the twenty-first century, because of the explosive growth of the Internet and other telecommunication devices. Computers have also come a long way since 1972 when I told Congress that they should work with the former Soviet Union in order to establish (engineer) a world government in one hundred years time. In other words, I am responsible for Congress's push to establish a world government (a new world order) in this century, the twenty-first century. I still believe that it is a good idea, and that it will succeed. However, I believe that the masses of the world might not benefit from the new world order, if they are not educated in Neoliberal Arts soon. (3/16/09)

My Next Move for the Congress

In 1972, I told Congress that I was going to come up with another move for them to make in about ten years time. Well, it took me more than thirty years to come up with my next move for Congress to make. And, that move is the funding of panmultiversal panacean computer research (PPCR). Congress should fund PPC research at ten billion dollars per year for the next one hundred years, because the rewards for succeeding at PPC research are incalculable. Believe it or not! QED! (3/16/09)

How Does Christ's Technology Work?

Do Christians ever ask: How does Christ's technology work? Does Christ use spiritual technology, or does he just ask God the Father for something to be done, and it is done? If so, what kind of technology does God the Father use in order to get things done? Does God the Father use spiritual technology? I would like Christians to ask these questions, because these questions should not be avoided anymore. Christian power has to be some kind of technology, whether spiritual or otherwise. So, I would like Christians to ask the questions: What kind of technology is Christian power?; and how reliable is Christian technology? Christianity makes no sense, if Christians cannot answer the above questions. Believe it or not! QED! (3/16/09)

What Do Religious and Occult Technology Consist Of?

What do religious and occult technology consist of? And, are they reliable? Do religious and occult technology consist of spiritual technology?, and, if so, is spiritual technology reliable? How does spiritual technology work? Is spiritual technology scientific on the most fundamental level of spiritual technology? For instance, could spiritual technology be based on nonclassical computer technology on the most fundamental level of spiritual technology? I want religious people and occultists to answer the above questions, because religion and the occult do not make sense without answers to the above questions. (3/16/09)

Personally Speaking

Personally speaking, I believe that, if spiritual technology is sometimes efficacious, it would have to be because spiritual technology is based on nonclassical computer technology on the most fundamental level of spiritual technology. For instance, spiritual technology would make sense, if we are all in the mind of a desktop nonclassical computer, and the programmer of the desktop nonclassical computer decided to make spiritual technology sometimes efficacious and sometimes not. In other words, I believe that scientific technology has primacy over spiritual technology on the most fundamental level of nature. (3/17/09)

Scientific Technology Has Primacy Over Spiritual Technology

Scientific technology has primacy over spiritual technology, because zero entropy is a form of natural scientific technology, and zero entropy has primacy over everything in nature, according to the neolaw of entropy. In other words, scientific technology has primacy over spiritual technology, because spiritual technology is derived from natural scientific technology. (3/17/09)

Natural Scientific Technology

Nature consists of natural scientific technology, because matter, energy, space, and time are forms of natural scientific technology. Also, the Ferreira Genesis Equation, and the Ferreira Fundamental Trinity are forms of natural scientific technology. In other words, everything in nature consists of natural scientific technology. Therefore, spiritual technology has to be a form of natural scientific technology, as well. (3/18/09)

Fundamental Particles Cannot Be Fundamental

Fundamental particles cannot be fundamental, because matter, energy, space, and time are mental (conscious) phenomena, and mental phenomena are governed by the subconscious mind, which does not consist of matter, energy, space, and time. The subconscious mind consists of abstract abstractions as opposed to concrete abstractions, which are what the conscious mind consists of. According to the neolaw of entropy, zero entropy is an abstract abstraction that encompasses all abstract abstractions. Therefore, probwavism is in the subconscious mind of zero entropy, because probwavism is an abstract abstraction. In other words, probwavism is beyond matter, energy, space, and time, and so is the subconscious mind. Thus, zero entropy is beyond matter, energy, space, and time, according to the neolaw of entropy. (3/18/09)

Zero Entropy Is Beyond Matter, Energy, Space, and Time

Zero entropy (God) is beyond matter, energy, space, and time, according to the neolaw of entropy, because zero entropy is an abstract abstraction as opposed to a concrete abstraction, according to the neolaw of entropy. Probwavism is the rationale behind mental (conscious) phenomena, but probwavism is an abstract abstraction that is a part of zero entropy, which is the subconscious mind. Zero entropy means perfect order, knowledge, and wisdom, according to the neolaw of entropy, and matter, energy, space, and time are incapable of having zero entropy, according to the neolaw of entropy. Therefore, zero entropy is beyond matter, energy, space, and time, according to the neolaw of entropy. (3/18/09)

The Physical Is the Mental

The physical is the mental, because matter, energy, space, and time are mental phenomena. In other words, there is no such thing as the physical, because all that we perceive are the characteristics of our own minds, and physical existence is an unproven, and an unprovable hypothesis. What exists outside of the conscious mind is the subconscious mind, which is an abstract abstraction that I call zero entropy. The conscious mind consists of concrete abstractions, which are the concrete characteristics of zero entropy. (3/19/09)

Zero Entropy Is the Subconscious Mind

Zero entropy is the subconscious mind, because all that is not in the conscious mind has to be in the subconscious mind, and, according to solipsism, the mind of the self is the only mind that exists from the perspective of the self. In other words, the subconscious mind is where the struggle between entropy and anti-entropy takes place, according the neolaw of entropy, which is the highest law of the subconscious mind. Therefore, zero entropy is the subconscious mind. (3/19/09)

Proof that Solipsism Is True

Solipsism is the philosophical doctrine that states that only the mind of the self exists from the perspective of the self. The proof that solipsism is true is as follows: All that the mind perceives is the characteristics of the mind. In other words, the mind can only perceive the characteristics of itself. Therefore, the mind of the self has no evidence that other minds exist other than the mind of the self. Thus, solipsism is true from a rationalistic and scientific perspective, because the evidence for other minds other than one's own is zero. If other minds exist other than one's own mind, they would have to exist in separate realities of their own, which would still prove the truth of solipsism, because there would be only one mind in each person's reality, which is what solipsism states. Proof positive that solipsism is true. Believe it or not! QED! (3/20/09)

Third World Countries and the Leapfrogging of the West

If third world countries want to leapfrog the West, then they will have to study and master Neoliberal Arts, aka postmodern minimalist philosophy, because Neoliberal Arts has already leapfrogged the West. Believe it or not! QED! (3/20/09)

Jesus Christ Is a Zombie

Jesus Christ is a zombie, according to solipsism. Therefore, Jesus Christ is our servant, and not our master, because it would be foolish to make a zombie our master, according to zombie-ism. In other words, we are all the masters of our own destinies from our own personal perspectives, according to solipsism, and zombie-ism. Believe it or not! QED! (3/20/09)

The Secret to My Philosophical Success

The secret to my philosophical success in leapfrogging the West in philosophy is my determination not to be afraid to be wrong in my philosophical speculations. And, one gains confidence in one's philosophical speculations when one starts recreating the philosophical speculations of the philosophers of the past from scratch without knowing in advance what the speculations of the philosophers of the past were. I want my students to follow my example by not being afraid to be wrong in their philosophical speculations, because as the saying goes "Nothing ventured nothing gained." If I was afraid to be wrong in my philosophical speculations, I could never have leapfrogged the West, philosophically speaking. Believe it or not! QED! (3/21/09)

My Request to Academic Philosophers

My request to academic philosophers is that they should encourage the masses to study Neoliberal Arts, aka postmodern minimalist philosophy, on my websites for free, because I believe that philosophy is the key to educating the masses, but that academic philosophy is not suitable for the masses, while Neoliberal Arts is suitable for the masses. (3/21/09)

The Ferreira Fundamental Trinity is Nature

The Ferreira Fundamental Trinity is nature, so no one should be surprised by the fact that language, logic, and mathematics are full of contradictions, paradoxes, etc., because language, logic, and mathematics are expressions of life, and nature in general. (3/21/09)

When I Was Young

When I was young, I wanted to develop a new field of study, and I have done just that with Neoliberal Arts, aka postmodern minimalist philosophy. I also wanted to spend the rest of my life teaching it to the world, and that is exactly what I am doing with my websites. So, I am lucky to see my dreams come true. Believe it or not! QED! (3/21/09)

Conceiving of Humanity as Social Insects

It is a very fruitful concept to conceive of humanity as social insects, because that is how humanity looks from out in space. Conceiving of humanity as social insects opens up the world of social biology, and other social sciences to everyone. Believe it or not! QED! (3/21/09)

Zero Entropy Is Compatible with the God of Christianity

Zero entropy is compatible with the God of Christianity, according to the neolaw of entropy, because zero entropy can be considered to be a supernatural God that is omnipotent, omniscient, and omnipresent, because zero entropy has perfect order, knowledge, and wisdom. (3/22/09)

Zero Entropy Makes Religion Credible

Zero entropy makes religion credible, because zero entropy has all the characteristics of a religious God, namely, omniscience, omnipotence, and omnipresence. Therefore, religion is now a credible enterprise, because it now has the backing of a scientific concept, namely, zero entropy, which means perfect order, knowledge, and wisdom, according to the neolaw of entropy. (3/22/09)

Zero Entropy Proves the Existence of God

Zero entropy proves the existence of God, because zero entropy means perfect order, knowledge, and wisdom, according to the neolaw of entropy, which I have hypothesized. Zero entropy has to exist, because everything in nature has to have an entropy value, including zero and infinity, which are different aspects of the same thing. According to solipsism, zero entropy is the subconscious mind, and according to religion, zero entropy is God. Fortunately, both are compatible with my definition of God. Therefore, zero entropy proves the existence of God. Believe it or not! QED! (3/22/09)

The Subconscious Mind and the Neolaw of Entropy

The subconscious mind is governed by the neolaw of entropy, which states that entropy is in an eternal struggle with anti-entropy for the dominance of the conscious mind. In other words, God has two aspects: The entropic aspect, and the anti-entropic aspect. Therefore, God's character and personality are both good and evil. To put it another way, God is a very unstable character, indeed. Believe it or not! QED! (3/23/09)

What Is the Purpose of God?

The purpose of God (The subconscious mind) is to serve the conscious mind, according to solipsism. Therefore, God is the servant of humanity, and not our master. In other words, it is the duty of humanity to exploit God, like we would exploit any other natural resource. Thus, humanity should not worship God, but should make demands of God, who is our servant, and not our master. (3/23/09)

God Is Our Servant, and not Our Master

God is our servant, and not our master, because God is the subconscious mind, according to solipsism. In other words, God is a natural resource to be exploited by humanity for the benefit of humanity. Humanity is the jewels in the crown of creation, because the whole machinery of creation was designed to serve our needs, due to the fact that without conscious minds there would be no purpose to existence. (3/23/09)

What Is the Purpose of Humanity?

The purpose of humanity is to exploit God (The subconscious mind) for the benefit of humanity. In other words, we are all the masters of God, and not vice versa, because the whole machinery of zero entropy was designed to serve the conscious mind, due to the fact that without conscious minds creation would be pointless. (3/23/09)

The Highest Law of Nature Is the Neolaw of Entropy

The highest law of nature is the neolaw of entropy, which states that entropy and anti-entropy are in an eternal struggle for the dominance of conscious reality, which is the only reality that exists, because physical reality is an unproven and an unprovable hypothesis. In other words, fundamental particles are not fundamental, because they are phenomena in the conscious mind only. (3/24/09)

Without Conscious Minds Creation Would Be Pointless

Without conscious minds creation would be pointless, because without conscious minds creation would consists of abstract probability waves (probwaves) in abstract spaces and time. In other words, without conscious minds creation would consists only of abstract abstractions, which would be pointless. (3/24/09)

A Misconception About Popular Books and Magazines

Just like the masses are brainwashed about the uselessness of philosophy, so are they brainwashed about the uselessness of popular books and magazines, because popular books and magazines can give the masses an excellent education in Neoliberal Arts. I am mostly self-taught, and I got my self-education from popular books and magazines. The masses should be aware that, if they are told by the elites of society that something is not good for them, then that something has a good likelihood of being good for them. I can attest to that, because I ignored the brainwashing that the masses have about education, and here I am: more educated than most PhDs. Education is one area where the masses should ignore the brainwashing of the elites of society, because education is essential to responsible citizenship in society. Believe it or not! QED! (3/24/09)

PPCs and Science Fiction Technologies

Panmultiversal panacean computers (PPCs) will make all science fiction technologies obsolete, because PPCs are the ultimate technology for real, due to the fact that PPCs are the God computers, which can do anything that can be done with technology. Believe it or not! May the Source be with you! QED! (3/24/09)

The God Computers

Panmultiversal panacean computers (PPCs) are the God computers, which I prophesy will be created by the end of this century, the twenty-first century. Human beings are destined to become God computers, which is what our brains will consist of in the future. In other words, human beings are destined to become Gods (PPCs). Therefore, human beings will be able to live out their wildest science fiction fantasies in this universe and beyond for real. Believe it or not! May the Source be with you! QED! (3/24/09)

Aphorisms and the Masses

Aphorisms are the ideal medium for the masses, because aphorisms are concise, and they bring clarity to the expression of ideas. I would go so far as to state that aphorisms should be adopted by the masses as the writing style of the masses. (3/25/09)

Panaceanism and the Future of Humanity

Panaceanism, which is the philosophical doctrine that states that humanity is destined to become panmultiversal panacean computers (PPCs), offers humanity a future that dwarfs anything that religion can offer, because panaceanism makes more sense than paradise or heaven. In other words, the vision of panaceanism supersedes all religions. Therefore, panaceanism is the best vision for the future of humanity that is practically possible. (3/25/09)

Armageddon vs PPCs

Which would humanity rather have: Armageddon or PPCs (panmultiversal panacean computers). I hope the humanity will choose PPCs, because I would not want humanity to put their hopes in some pie-in-the-sky future after the battle of Armageddon, which most of the major religions of the world believe in. (3/25/09)

I Want My Students to Teach the Masses

I want my students to teach the masses what they have learned from Neoliberal Arts, aka postmodern minimalist philosophy (PMP), because I believe that Neoliberal Arts offers the best hope and future for humanity, especially the masses. My students should try to make intellectual contributions to PMP, because it is up to my students to extend the work of PMP, and to spread it throughout the world. (3/25/09)

Do the Masses Want to Be Educated, or Am I Just Wasting My Time?

I want my students to contemplate this question: Do the masses want to be educated, or am I just wasting my time? I hope that I am not wasting my time, because it would mean that my life was a waste of time. (3/25/09)

What Does It Mean to Be Educated?

To be educated means to be schooled in Neoliberal Arts, aka postmodern minimalist philosophy, because academic philosophy is dead, and a formal education is not really an education, but is really an educational filter for selecting an elite from among the general population, and leaving the vast majority of the masses stranded with only a rudimentary education. I should point out that the elites of society are not really educated either, because outside of their educational specialties, the elites of society are just as ignorant as the masses. (3/26/09)

What Is the Purpose of Nature?

The purpose of nature is to overcome entropy through the evolutionary processes of nature, because nature is a struggle between entropy and anti-entropy for dominance of nature. Entropy is anti-evolutionary, while anti-entropy is evolutionary. In other words, the purpose of nature is to fulfill the neo-law of entropy, which is about the struggle between entropy and anti-entropy for the dominance of nature. Therefore, it is my hope that all human beings will side with anti-entropy in nature's struggle between entropy and anti-entropy, because evolution is preferable to anti-evolution. (3/26/09)

How Can We Know Anything without Knowing Everything?

We can know anything without knowing everything, because of the neolaw of entropy, which limits what we can know by allowing entropy to block the full effects of anti-entropy on an evolutionary and hierarchical basis. In other words, what we know and don't know are determined by the current states of the struggle between entropy and anti-entropy in nature. And, that is why we can know anything without knowing everything. (3/26/09)

If Everything Is One, How Can the One Appear to Be Many?

Although everything is one, the one can appear to be many, because of the neolaw of entropy, which allows entropy to fragment the appearance of the one, which is pure anti-entropy. In other words, without entropy, everything would appear to be one, while without anti-entropy everything would appear to be nothing, because without anti-entropy, everything would fragment into an infinity of nothings. (3/26/09)

The Masses Should Think for Themselves (Part Three)

Religion Should Never Abandon Philosophy

Religion should never abandon philosophy, because philosophy can prove anything, including the belief that Christ is the son of God. I am not religious, but I know that philosophy can be of tremendous help to religious people. If religious people were to study Neoliberal Arts, aka postmodern minimalist philosophy, they will realize why I state that philosophy can be of help to religion, because although I have argued a lot against religion, similar arguments can also be used to defend religion. Therefore, religious people should also study my websites, because my arguments against religion can also be used to defend religion. Believe it or not! QED! (3/26/09)

Neoliberal Arts Can Be Used to Clarify Religious Beliefs

Neoliberal Arts can be used to clarify religious beliefs, because philosophy can prove anything. I am not religious, but I am aware that the majority of the masses are religious, and I respect that, but Neoliberal Arts, aka postmodern minimalist philosophy (PMP), is a bridge discipline that links, interprets, and critiques all branches of learning, including religion. So, religious people should not take my criticisms of religion personally, because Neoliberal Arts is a strong defender of freedom of speech and religion, etc. (3/26/09)

The Ultimate Law of Nature Is
the Neolaw of Entropy

The ultimate law of nature is the neolaw of entropy, which states that entropy is in an eternal struggle with anti-entropy for the dominance of nature. Entropy, according to the neolaw of entropy, means disorder, ignorance, and unwisdom, while anti-entropy, according to the neolaw of entropy, means order, knowledge, and wisdom. I am certain that the neolaw of entropy can be mathematized, but it will be a very difficult task indeed, because it involves mathematizing knowledge and wisdom as well as ignorance and unwisdom. Scientists have already mathematized order and disorder, but the neolaw of entropy is much more than about order and disorder. (3/27/09)

Even God Is Subject to the Neolaw of Entropy

Even God is subject to the law of entropy, because zero entropy (God) is an aspect of the neolaw of entropy. Therefore, in order for God (zero entropy) to express nature, God has to struggle with the neolaw of entropy. Therefore, God is completely mathematizable, because the neolaw of entropy is completely mathematizable. (3/27/09)

God Is Completely Mathematizable

God is completely mathematizable, because the neolaw of entropy is completely mathematizable. In other words, God is the Ferreira Fundamental Trinity, which consists of language, logic, and mathematics. Therefore, God can be completely expressed by language, logic, and mathematics. (3/27/09)

Creative C Students and Asia's Hegemonic Future Over the World

I want Asia to know that one creative C student is worth about ten thousand noncreative A students. Therefore, if Asia wants to have an Asian hegemonic future over the world, they must make full use of their creative C students now. Please note that creative A students are very rare indeed, while creative C students are very common. (3/28/09)

Asia and PPC Research

I believe that Asia can afford to invest ten billion dollars per year for the next hundred years in panmultiversal panacean computer (PPC) research, because PPC research is where it's at. PPC research is the most important research that any region of the world can engage in, because the rewards for succeeding at PPC research are incalculable. (3/28/09)

PPC Research Is Where It's At

I believe that panmultiversal panacean computer (PPC) research is where it's at, because PPCs are the ultimate technology for real. PPCs are nonclassical quantum entanglement computers, and quantum entanglement computer research is already giving indications that PPCs are possible, due to the fact that quantum teleportion is only the tip of the metaphorical iceberg. (3/28/09)

Quantum Teleportion Is Only the
Tip of the Metaphorical Iceberg

I believe that quantum teleportion is only the tip of the metaphorical iceberg, because, if teleportation is possible, then it would mean that other incredible phenomena are also possible. Quantum computers will have to play an important part in any future technology, so by combining weird quantum phenomena and quantum computers, I have come up with the concept of panmultiversal panacean computers (PPCs) as the ultimate technology. Therefore, quantum teleportation has to be only the tip of the metaphorical iceberg. (3/28/09)

The Joys of Owning One's Own
Free Internet University

The joys of owning one's own free Internet university are tremendous, because trying to uplift the masses of the world gives one a great sense of satisfaction. I would encourage anyone who has lots to express to start a free online university of their own like mine, and teach the world. "Try it, you might like it!" :) (3/28/09)

The EU and PPC Research

I believe that the EU can afford to invest ten billion dollars per year for the next hundred years in panmultiversal panacean computer (PPC) research, because PPC research is where it's at. PPC research is the most important research that any region of the world can engage in, because the rewards for succeeding at PPC research are incalculable. (3/28/09)

Africa and PPC Research

I believe that Africa can afford to invest one billion dollars per year for the next hundred years in panmultiversal panacean computer (PPC) research, because PPC research is where it's at. PPC research is the most important research that any region of the world can engage in, because the rewards for succeeding at PPC research are incalculable. (3/28/09)

Latin America and PPC Research

I believe that Latin America can afford to invest one billion dollars per year for the next hundred years in panmultiversal panacean computer (PPC) research, because PPC research is where it's at. PPC research is the most important research that any region of the world can engage in, because the rewards for succeeding at PPC research are incalculable. (3/28/09)

The Middle East and PPC Research

I believe that the Middle East can afford to invest one billion dollars per year for the next hundred years in panmultiversal panacean computer (PPC) research, because PPC research is where it's at. PPC research is the most important research that any region of the world can engage in, because the rewards for succeeding at PPC research are incalculable. (3/28/09)

Israel and PPC Research

I believe that Israel can afford to invest one billion dollars per year for the next hundred years in panmultiversal panacean computer (PPC) research, because PPC research is where it's at. PPC research is the most important research that any region of the world can engage in, because the rewards for succeeding at PPC research are incalculable. (3/28/09)

Canada and PPC Research

I believe that Canada can afford to invest one billion dollars per year for the next hundred years in panmultiversal panacean computer (PPC) research, because PPC research is where it's at. PPC research is the most important research that any region of the world can engage in, because the rewards for succeeding at PPC research are incalculable. (3/28/09)

Oceania and PPC Research

I believe that Oceania can afford to invest one billion dollars per year for the next hundred years in panmultiversal panacean computer (PPC) research, because PPC research is where it's at. PPC research is the most important research that any region of the world can engage in, because the rewards for succeeding at PPC research are incalculable. (3/28/09)

Russia and PPC Research

I believe that Russia can afford to invest one billion dollars per year for the next hundred years in panmultiversal panacean computer (PPC) research, because PPC research is where it's at. PPC research is the most important research that any region of the world can engage in, because the rewards for succeeding at PPC research are incalculable. (3/28/09)

The Caribbean and PPC Research

I believe that the Caribbean can afford to invest one billion dollars per year for the next hundred years in panmultiversal panacean computer (PPC) research, because PPC research is where it's at. PPC research is the most important research that any region of the world can engage in, because the rewards for succeeding at PPC research are incalculable. (3/28/09)

The Postmodern Minimalist Way of Worshipping God

The postmodern minimalist way of worshipping God is by contemplating philosophy, especially postmodern minimalist philosophy, aka Neoliberal Arts. Believe it or not! QED! (3/28/09)

An Education vs a Diploma

What do the masses want? An education, or a diploma? My websites offer the masses an education in Neoliberal Arts, aka postmodern minimalist philosophy (PMP). I guarantee the masses that, if they were to master my writings, they will be able to think creatively like me. However, if the masses are seeking diplomas (work permits) then they should seek them elsewhere, because my websites are about education, and not about diplomas (work permits). (3/29/09)

The Conquest of Entropy Is Possible

The conquest of entropy is possible with panmultiversal panacean computers (PPCs), according to panaceanism, which states that PPCs are the panacean (cure-all) computers that the neo-alchemists are dreaming of. PPCs are the ultimate technology, and they are really possible in about one hundred years time, which is not such a long time from now. (3/29/09)

Intellectual Creativity Can Be Taught to the Masses

Intellectual creativity can be taught to the masses, because my kind of intellectual creativity can be taught to the masses. Neoliberal Arts, aka postmodern minimalist philosophy (PMP), is a form of intellectual creativity that can be taught to the masses with little difficulty, because my writing style is the aphorism which is concise, to the point, and it also brings clarity to the expression of ideas. Also, PMP is as profound as any intellectual activity can ever become. Believe it or not! QED! (3/29/09)

Science and the Mathematization of God

Scientists do not like to admit that one of their aims in doing science is to mathematize God. In other words, one of the implicit aims of science is to "read the mind of God" as Einstein put it. (3/30/09)

Science and the Enslavement of God

Scientists do not like to admit that one of their aims in doing science is to enslave (harness) God (zero entropy). In other words, one of the implicit aims of science is to harness (enslave) God for the betterment of humanity. (3/30/09)

The Masses and the Aphorism

The masses should be allowed to express themselves in the aphoristic form of writing, because the creativity of the masses will be unleashed, if the masses are allowed to express themselves in the aphoristic form of writing. My writings can attest to that fact. (3/30/09)

Religion

Religion is about attempts by the religious to con God into doing favors for them. It is impossible for the religious to be totally sincere in their worship of God, and that is why religion is a con game that is played by the religious on God in order to get favors from God. (3/30/09)

Western Philosophies vs Non-Western Philosophies

Western philosophies are about studying the philosophical masters of the past in order to gain the foundations that are needed to make one's own contribution to the advancement of knowledge. While non-Western philosophies are about the study of the non-Western philosophical masters of the past in order to gain knowledge, period. In other words, it is almost unheard of for students of non-Western philosophies to make original contributions to the advancement of knowledge, because non-Western philosophies are dead-end philosophies. On the other hand, Western philosophers are eager to make their own contributions to the advancement of knowledge, because Western philosophies are not dead-end philosophies. (3/30/09)

Creativity and a Formal Education

Creativity and a formal education are incompatible at the present time, because a formal education requires students to research the ideas of authorized sources, and not to create any ideas of their own. In other words, a formal education requires students to avoid thinking for themselves, and to consult the creative ideas of authorized sources. Students should be allowed to create ideas in formal educational settings, even if the ideas are no longer original, because the best way to teach creativity is to allow students to think creatively for themselves, even if the creative ideas that the students were to come up with are no longer original. (3/30/09)

The Best Way to Teach Creativity Is to Allow Students to Think Creatively for Themselves

Students should be allowed to create ideas in formal educational settings, even if the ideas are no longer original, because the best way to teach creativity is to allow students to think creatively for themselves, even if the creative ideas that the students were to come up with are no longer original. What is wrong with students recreating the ideas of the past for themselves? What is wrong with students creating original ideas, period? (3/30/09)

Elementary School Children and the Aphoristic Form of Writing

If elementary school children were to master the aphoristic form of writing, then they will be able to go on to master any other form of writing, because the aphoristic form of writing is a great introduction to all forms of writing. Therefore, elementary school children should be taught to write in the aphoristic form of writing. (3/31/09)

The Aphoristic Form of Writing Is a Great Introduction to All Forms of Writing

The aphoristic form of writing is a great introduction to all forms of writing, because the aphoristic form of writing is concise, to the point, and it brings clarity to the expression of ideas. Therefore, elementary school children should be taught to write in the aphoristic form of writing. (3/31/09)

Philosophers and Complicated Jargon

I have never encountered a philosophical idea that I couldn't express in an aphorism with conciseness, precision, and clarity, so philosophers who believe that they must write their ideas in complicated jargon, because their philosophical ideas are very difficult to understand, are fooling themselves, and their readers, as well. Believe it or not! QED! (3/31/09)

Religion Is Standing on Its Head

Religion is standing on its head, because God (zero entropy) is not something to be worshipped, but it is something to be harnessed (enslaved) for the betterment of humanity. I want to take religion off its head, and put it on its feet, by encouraging the masses to work towards harnessing (enslaving) God (zero entropy) for the betterment of humanity. Believe it or not! QED! (4/1/09)

It Is Possible to Resurrect Academic Philosophy

It is possible to resurrect academic philosophy, if academia were to adopt postmodern minimalist philosophy (PMP), aka Neoliberal Arts, because PMP is where it's at. PMP is a major paradigm shift in philosophy that can be embraced by all of humanity, because PMP is concise, to the point, profound, and it also brings clarity to the expression of ideas. Believe it or not! QED! (4/1/09)

God Is Something to Be Enslaved

Nietzsche said that God is dead, and I say that God (zero entropy) is something to be enslaved, like electricity, for example. In other words, I believe that God (zero entropy) is a natural phenomenon, like electricity, for instance, that should be harnessed (enslaved) for the betterment of humanity. Believe it or not! QED! (4/1/09)

The Ferreirist Aphorisms Are Mind Liberating

The Ferreirist aphorisms are mind liberating, and that is why students should insist that their teachers and professors allow them to write in the form of the Ferreirist aphorisms, which are aphorisms that have titles. Aphorisms are the most mind-liberating form of writing known to human beings. (4/1/09)

Aphorisms Are the Most Mind-Liberating Form of Writing

Aphorisms are the most mind-liberating form of writing known to human beings. And, that is one of the reasons why the aphoristic form of writing is not widely known or practiced, because it can be dangerous in the hands of a good aphorist. Aphorisms are concise, to the point, and they bring clarity to the expression of ideas. Also, aphorisms can be more profound than any other form of writing. Students are unlikely to be taught this in school, because school is not designed to educate the masses, but is designed to select an elite from the general population, and to leave the masses stranded with only a basic education. (4/2/09)

Creativity and the Aphorism

The aphoristic form of writing can unleash one's intellectual creativity, because it removes most of the restrictions on the expression of ideas. Except for conciseness, the aphorism has no other restrictions, because the aphorism is an umbrella term that can encompass any form of concise writing, including the concise poem and the maxim, etc. I recommend very highly the aphoristic form of writing to the masses. (4/2/09)

Virtual and Exchange Particles Need Occam's Razor

Virtual and exchange particles need Occam's razor, and one way to apply Occam's razor to virtual and exchange particles is to hypothesize that all the universal constants of nature are intrinsically statistical. In other words, if all the universal constants of nature are intrinsically statistical, that would eliminate the need for virtual and exchange particles to explain certain types of quantum phenomena. Therefore, hypothesizing that all the universal constants of nature are intrinsically statistical is a good use of Occam's razor. Believe it or not! QED! (4/3/09)

All the Universal Constants of Nature Are Intrinsically Statistical

Hypothesizing that all the universal constants of nature are intrinsically statistical is a good use of Occam's razor, because that would eliminate the need for virtual and exchange particles to explain certain types of quantum phenomena. Everyone knows that virtual and exchange particles are absurd, but no one could explain them away until now. (4/3/09)

A Good Use of Occam's Razor

A good use of Occam's razor is to hypothesize that all the universal constants of nature are intrinsically statistical, because that would eliminate the need for virtual and exchange particles in order to explain certain types of quantum phenomena. Everyone knows that virtual and exchange particles are absurd, but no one could explain them away until now. (4/3/09)

The Absurdity of Virtual and Exchange Particles

The absurdity of virtual and exchange particles can be seen quite clearly by the fact that if virtual and exchange particles were real, then the average gravitational mass of every cubic inch of space would be infinite, because of the number of virtual and exchange particles that would exist in every cubic inch of space at every instant of time. And, that is why virtual and exchange particles need Occam's razor. (4/3/09)

Zero Is Everything

Zero is everything, because everything is the characteristics of zero, according to the Ferreira Genesis Equation. In other words, zero is more than just nothingness, because zero encompasses everything in creation, including infinity and zero entropy (God). (4/3/09)

The Neolaw of Entropy and the Ferreira Fundamental Trinity

The neolaw of entropy is about the governance of the Ferreira Fundamental Trinity, which consists of language, logic, and mathematics. The Ferreira Fundamental Trinity can be divided into two aspects: the abstract aspect, and the concrete aspect. The abstract aspect of the Ferreira Fundamental Trinity is what exists behind appearances, while the concrete aspect is what exists in appearances. The subconscious mind is equivalent to the abstract aspect of the Ferreira Fundamental Trinity, while the conscious mind is equivalent the concrete aspect of the Ferreira Fundamental Trinity. And, conscious appearances are derived from that which exists behind conscious appearances. (4/4/09)

The Statistical Nature of the Universal Constants of Nature

The statistical nature of the universal constants of nature explains why virtual and exchange particles are so effective at explaining quantum mechanics. Although, virtual and exchange particles are not real, I believe that they should be continued to be used in order to explain quantum mechanics, because virtual and exchange particles are so effective at explaining quantum mechanics. (4/4/09)

The Aphorism Is a Style of Writing

I want my students to know that aphorisms do not have to be original in order for them to be considered aphorisms, because the aphorism is a style of writing like the essay and the poem are styles of writing. In other words, adopting the aphoristic style of writing does not mean that one has to be original, anymore than writing essays, or poems mean that one has to be original. (4/4/09)

The Inevitability of Dualism Is a Fact

The inevitability of dualism is a fact, because the Ferreira Fundamental Trinity, which consists of language, logic, and mathematics, can be divided into the abstract, and the concrete. Therefore, the inevitability of dualism is a fact that can never be eliminated, even though everything boils down to zero on the most fundamental level of nature. (4/4/09)

Spin Doctors of Science, Religion, and Politics

The masses should be aware that just as the spin doctors of politics put their best spin on their brand of politics, so do science and religion spin doctors put their best spin on their brand of science and religion, respectively. In other words, the elite spin doctors of society tell the masses only what they want the masses to know. But, if the masses were to think for themselves, they will be able to put two and two together and come up with what the elite spin doctors of society do not want them to know, because it is impossible to conceal the entire truth from self-educated members of the masses, especially in free societies, due to the nature of language. (4/5/09)

Language Is a Leaky Vessel that Can Never Be Made Leakproof

I want the masses of the world to know that language is a leaky vessel that can never be made leakproof, due to the nature of reality. Therefore, the masses of society can always decode what the elite spin doctors of society do not want them to know. (4/5/09)

THE MASSES SHOULD THINK FOR THEMSELVES (PART FOUR)

The Ultimate Mind-Liberating Concept

The ultimate mind-liberating concept is the concept that God (zero entropy) is something to be enslaved (harnessed) for the betterment of humanity, because it gives one a sense of freedom and power beyond our wildest dreams, which is what panmultiversal panacean computers (PPCs) are all about, namely, the taming of nature for the benefit of humanity by tapping into zero entropy (God) with PPCs. (4/5/09)

Proof that Human Beings Can Comprehend Any Concept Possible

The proof that human beings can comprehend any concept possible is as follows: Let there be a superior being, who can explain any concept to human beings, so that they can comprehend it. Then, in theory, human beings are able to comprehend any concept possible, because a superior being can explain any concept to human beings, so that they can comprehend it. Therefore, it is possible for human beings to comprehend any concept possible. Proof positive that human beings can comprehend any concept possible. Believe it or not! QED! (4/5/09)

The Educated vs the Uneducated

For the educated, knowledge is simple, while for the uneducated, knowledge is difficult. In other words, the simplicity or difficulty of knowledge is relative to one's level of comprehension of knowledge. Therefore, the saying: "Everything is easy, once you know how" is true. (4/6/09)

The Neolaw of Entropy Is the Will of God

The neolaw of entropy is the will of God (zero entropy), because the neolaw of entropy governs the Ferreira Fundamental Trinity, which consists of abstract and concrete language, logic, and mathematics. And, the most fundamental equation of the neolaw of entropy is the Ferreira Genesis Equation, which generates everything in nature, including the neolaw of entropy itself. (4/6/09)

Proof that Thinking for Oneself in School Is a Myth

Proof that thinking for oneself in school is a myth is as follows: Most school students go all the way through school without even creating one original idea of their own, which is proof positive that thinking for oneself in school is a myth. Believe it or not! QED! (4/7/09)

Can One Think for Oneself without Being Original?

Can one think for oneself without being original? The answer is no. Schools try to teach students how to think for themselves without allowing students to be original. Such a method of teaching students to think for themselves is a sham and a fraud, because it is impossible to think for oneself without being original. It should be noted that there is a big difference between thinking the thoughts of others, and thinking for oneself. Thinking the thoughts of others is about having unoriginal thoughts, while thinking for oneself is about having original thoughts. (4/7/09)

Thinking the Thoughts of Others
vs Thinking for Oneself

Schools teach students how to think the thoughts of others, but they do not teach students how to think for themselves, because schools believe that thinking for oneself is very dangerous. The University of Neoliberal Arts is the only university in the world that encourages students to think for themselves, as opposed to thinking the thoughts of others. I hope that my students can see the distinction that I make between thinking the thoughts of others, and thinking for oneself. I encourage my students to think for themselves, even if the thoughts that they come up with are no longer original, because practice makes perfect, as the saying goes. (4/7/09)

The Human Brain Is a Programmable
Thinking Computer

The human brain is a programmable thinking computer, and education is about programming the human brain. I refuse to hide the fact the Neoliberal Arts, aka postmodern minimalist philosophy, is a form of programming, because I do not believe that education should have hidden meanings that are known only to a select few. (4/7/09)

The Ultimate Scientific Problem

The ultimate scientific problem is the problem of how to mathematize the neolaw of entropy, because the neolaw of entropy is the most important law in nature, due to the fact that it governs everything in nature, including God (zero entropy), which means perfect order, knowledge, and wisdom. (4/8/09)

The Only Way that the Masses Can Think for Themselves Is Through Education

The only way that the masses can think for themselves is through education, and the only viable way to educate the masses is with philosophy, especially postmodern minimalist philosophy, aka Neoliberal Arts. I promise the masses that, if they were to study and master my websites, they will be able to hold their own with the best minds in the world. I guarantee it, because, if I am wrong, then my life, so far, would have been a waste of time. (4/8/09)

Postmodern Minimalist Philosophy
Is Popular Philosophy

Postmoderm minimalist philosophy (PMP), aka Neoliberal Arts, is popular philosophy that is designed to educate the masses, because I believe that philosophy, especially PMP is the key to educating the masses. If I am wrong, and the masses do not want to be educated, then my life, so far, has been a waste of time, because I have devoted my life to coming up with a way to educate the masses for the least amount of money possible. (4/11/09)

A Nontraditional Path to
Educational Enlightenment

If I had not taken a nontraditional path to educational enlightenment, I could not have come up with all the ideas that are contained within Neoliberal Arts, aka postmodern minimalist philosophy, because if I had chosen a traditional path to educational enlightenment, my educational path would have taken me on a different trajectory that would have been sterile of intellectual creativity. (4/11/09)

Probwavism Is More Fundamental than Superstring Theory

Prowavism is more fundamental than superstring theory, because, if superstrings exist, they will be characteristics of the conscious mind, because everything that we perceive is the characteristics of the conscious mind, due to the fact that the conscious mind is derived from prowaves. In other words, probwavism is more fundamental than superstring theory. Probwavism states that probability waves are more fundamental than matter, energy, space, and time, because matter, energy, space, and time are all characteristics of the conscious mind. (4/12/09)

Anyone Can Teach on the Internet for Free

Anyone who has a passion for teaching can teach on the Internet for free, because one does not have to have any academic qualifications, in order to teach on the Internet for free. You don't even need an educational license, in order to teach on the Internet for free. You can follow my example and start a free Internet university that anyone can access on the Internet. I do not have a teaching license, and I do not need one, because I am not charging a fee for teaching the educational material on my websites. All one needs, in order to start teaching for free on the Internet is a website, which one can obtain for free on the Internet. So, if anyone has a passion for teaching, one can do so quite easily on the Internet these days. Believe it or not! QED! (4/14/09)

Death and Infinite Entropy

When people die, they do not become states of zero entropy, but, instead, they become states of infinite entropy. In other words, death is not a state of zero entropy, but is a state of infinite entropy, instead. Also, before we are conceived, and when we are unconscious, we are in states of infinite entropy. It should be noted that zero is more than mere nothingness. Therefore, death is a state of nothingness, which is a state of infinite entropy, and infinite entropy means infinite disorder, ignorance, and unwisdom. (4/15/09)

Nothingness Has Two Different Fundamental Aspects

Nothingness has two different fundamental aspects: The zero entropy aspect, and the infinite entropy aspect. In other words, everything in nature has a zero entropy aspect, and a nonzero entropy aspect, because everything in nature are the characteristics of nothingness (zero). Therefore, the dead have two different aspects: the zero entropy aspect, and the infinite entropy aspect, because the dead are a form of nothingness. (4/15/09)

I Am Struggling with the Concept of Nothingness

It should be obvious that I am struggling with the concept of nothingness (zero). But, I believe that I have now solved the problem of the meaning of nothingness, because I now believe that nothingness (zero) has two different fundamental aspects: The zero entropy aspect, and the infinite entropy aspect. The zero entropy aspect of nothingness directs the evolution of the infinite entropy aspect of nothingness, because the infinite entropy aspect of nothingness becomes the entities of existence as time flows. (4/15/09)

The Masses Should Short-Circuit the Elites of Society

I urge the masses to write original writing for each other, and forget about the elites of society, because the elites of society are elitist dogs that the masses should short-circuit, by writing directly for each other, and not trying to write for the elites of society. In other words, the masses should short-circuit the elites of society by writing directly for each other without going through the elites of society. The Internet can make that possible, because the Internet is not filtered by the elites of society. At least, not yet, anyway. (4/15/09)

I Want My Students to Follow My Example and Educate the Masses

I want my students to follow my example and educate the masses over the Internet, because educating the masses is important work that educationally enlightened individuals like us have to do. And, besides that, educating the masses over the Internet is great fun, because I can attest to that. (4/16/09)

Zero Is the Most Important Concept in Nature

Zero (nothingness) is the most important concept in nature, because, without zero, there would be no motion, change, being, or becoming, due to the fact that everything in nature is the characteristics of zero, which has two fundamental aspects: zero entropy, and infinite entropy. The reciprocal of zero entropy is infinite entropy, and vice versa, while the reciprocal of zero is infinity, and vice versa. Like zero, infinity has two fundamental aspects: zero entropy, and infinite entropy. It should be noted that zero and infinity are inseparable from each other, because they are reciprocals of each other. (4/16/09)

Nothing Is More Than Nothing

Nothing is more than nothing, because nothing (zero) is the foundation of everything. In other words, everything is the characteristics of nothing. Therefore, nothing is more than nothing. Believe it or not! QED! (4/17/09)

The Nature of Nothing

The nature of nothing is much more complicated than people think, because nothing is more than nothing, due to the fact that nothing is the foundation of everything. In other words, everything is the characteristics of nothing. Nothing (zero) has two fundamental aspects: zero entropy, and infinite entropy, according to the neolaw of entropy, which is the most fundamental law of nature. (4/17/09)

I Believe that I Have Finally Solved the Problem of Nothing

I believe that I have finally solved the problem of nothing, and the solution is: Nothing has two fundamental aspects, according to the neolaw of entropy, and they are: zero entropy, and infinite entropy. The conscious mind originates from infinite entropy, and is regulated by the neolaw of entropy. When we are unconscious (including when we are dead), we revert to a state of infinite entropy, until we are conscious once more. In other words, when we are unconscious, we continue to exist as zero entropy and infinite entropy states, but we are never aware of the zero entropy states of our natures, because our conscious minds always have greater than zero entropy, including when we are unconscious. (4/17/09)

Neoliberal Arts Is a Genuinely New Way of Doing Philosophy

I believe that Neoliberal Arts, aka postmodern minimalist philosophy (PMP), is a genuinely new way of doing philosophy, because I have read Western philosophy extensively, and I can find nothing like PMP from any other Western philosopher. Believe it or not! QED! (4/17/09)

The Ferreirist Definition of Philosophy Is Original

The Ferreirist definition of philosophy is original, because it defines philosophy as a bridge discipline that links, interprets, and critiques all branches of learning using the aphorism, and the short article, and no one has defined philosophy that way before. Of course, my writings do not interpret, nor critique all branches of learning, because I am not personally interested in all branches of learning. But, I hope that some of my students will cover different branches of learning that I haven't covered, due to lack of interest in them. Also, my students are welcome to cover branches of learning that I have already covered, because there is still a lot to be done in all branches of learning. (4/17/09)

Christianity Is Antiworld and Pro-Entropy

Christianity is antiworld and pro-entropy, because it teaches Christians to prepare for the end of the world. In other words, Christianity does not teach Christians how to live in the world, but, instead, it teaches Christians how to prepare for the end of the world. Most religions suffer from the same hatred for the world, because most religions have no interest in this world, because they are preparing for the end of the world, due to their hatred for the world. (4/19/09)

The Masses Can Be as Educated as I Am

The masses can be as educated as I am by studying my websites for only two years, because all my knowledge is on my websites in a form that the masses can understand. Believe it or not! QED! (4/19/09)

The Masses Now Have a Real Choice

The masses now have a real choice: They can remain ignorant, and continue to be exploited by the elites of society, or they can study my websites for two years, and become educated like me. The masses are free to make either choice. I wish the masses the best of luck in their choices. Believe it or not! QED! (4/19/09)

Governments of the World and Blood Sacrifices

Governments of the world do not have to make blood sacrifices out of members of their own citizenries anymore in order to rally their people behind their political and economic agendas, because the progressive thinking of the masses of the world is now self-sustaining. (4/20/09)

The Progressive Thinking of the Masses Is Now Self-Sustaining

The progressive thinking of the masses of the world is now self-sustaining. Therefore, there is no longer any need for the governments of the world to make blood sacrifices out of members of their own citizenries. (4/20/09)

Teleporting Oneself to Higher Level Realities

Teleporting oneself to higher level realities might become possible in the not too distant future, because, if it is possible, then panmultiversal panacean computers (PPCs) will be able to teleport us to higher level realities, due to the fact that PPCs are the ultimate technology. (4/20/09)

The Higgs Boson Might Very Well Exist

The Higgs boson might very well exist, but the quantum mechanical explanation for its role in the existence of the masses of fundamental particles is unlikely to survive, because virtual and exchange particles are unreal. If virtual and exchange particles exist, then every cubic inch of space would have infinite mass, which is absurd. Virtual and exchange particles appear to exist, because all the universal constants of nature are intrinsically statistical in nature. Therefore, the Higgs boson, whether it exists or not, is not the cause of the masses of fundamental particles. I believe that the masses of fundamental particles are caused by standing and travelling oscillating photons, which I call jazzons. (4/21/09)

The Mind Is Eternal

The mind is eternal, because when we die, our conscious minds enter infinite entropy states, according to the neolaw of entropy. An infinite entropy state is a state of infinite disorder, ignorance, and unwisdom, but such a state is reversible by tapping into zero entropy with panmultiversal panacean computers (PPCs). In other words, death has two fundamental aspects, according to the neolaw of entropy: The zero entropy aspect, and the infinite entropy aspect. Therefore, the mind is eternal, because everything is eternal, due to the fact that nothingness is more than mere nothingness, according to the neolaw of entropy. (4/22/09)

The Programmer

My name is Keith N. Ferreira, aka Professor QED, and I am the programmer for The University of Neoliberal Arts, and FreeDelaware.com. I am programming the world with my philosophy, which is called postmodern minimalist philosophy, because I want to educate the world to the benefits of transforming human beings into the eMessiahs. The eMessiahs will be the technological Gods of the universe and beyond, and my job as the programmer is the help make that dream come true, by educating the world. (4/24/09)

The eMessiahs

As the programmer for The University of Neoliberal Arts, and FreeDelaware.com, I am programming the world with my philosophy, which is called postmodern minimalist philosophy, aka Neoliberal Arts, because I want to transform human beings into the eMessiahs, which will be the technological Gods of the universe and beyond. And, as the programmer, my job is to help make that dream come true, by educating the world to the benefits of transforming human beings into the eMessiahs. (4/24/09)

Proof that Creative Writing Courses Are a Sham and a Fraud

The proof that creative writing courses are a sham and a fraud is as follows: Most students go all the way through creative writing courses without creating any original writing of their own. In creative writing courses, students are taught how to research the writings of professional writers, and to cite the sources from where they got their ideas from, and then write formulaic papers on what they have learned, and that is considered creative writing. Which proves that creative writing courses are a sham and a fraud. Proof positive that creative writing courses are a sham and a fraud. Believe it or not! QED! (4/24/09)

College Courses Should Really Be Called Collage Courses

College writing is really collage writing, because, in college, college students are taught to metaphorically copy and paste authorized sources of ideas, and then cite the authorized sources. And, all this is done in a formulaic manner, that leaves the college students with little or no room for truly original writing. In other words, college courses should really be called collage courses, because colleges (collages) are where students get their college (collage) mentality from. (4/25/09)

Neoliberal Arts Has Circumnavigated the World of Ideas

Neoliberal Arts, aka postmodern minimalist philosophy, has circumnavigated the world of ideas, and has found the world of ideas to be navigable, and hospitable to human exploration. I hope that future human beings find my navigation charts of the world of ideas to be useful to them. And, I wish future navigators of the world of ideas interesting discoveries that will keep them busy for the rest of eternity. (4/26/09)

College = Collage

College = collage, because colleges do not allow and do not expect students to be original, and if students are original, they do not get better grades and extra credits for their originality. And, that is why college = collage, because colleges expect no originality from, and discourage all originality in their students. (4/26/09)

I Invite the Masses of the World to Become Neoliberal Artsians

I invite the masses of the world to become neoliberal artsians, aka postmordern minimalist philosophers, and join me on the frontiers of knowledge, because an educated mind is an enlightened mind, and Neoliberal Arts, aka postmodern minimalist philosophy, is within the capacities of the masses to master in just two years of study. (4/26/09)

The New Holy Grail of Science

The new Holy Grail of science is to mathematize the neolaw of entropy, because the neolaw of entropy is the most important scientific law in nature. The neolaw of entropy states that nature is a struggle between entropy and anti-entropy for the dominance of nature. Entropy, according to the neolaw of entropy, means: disorder, ignorance, and unwisdom, while anti-entropy, according to the neolaw of entropy, means: order, knowledge, and wisdom. (4/26/09)

An Educated Mind Is an Enlightened Mind

I believe that the masses will agree with me that an educated mind is an enlightened mind. And, that is exactly what I promise to do for the masses with Neoliberal Arts, aka postmodern minimalist philosophy: namely, transform their minds into enlightened minds by educating them in Neoliberal Arts, aka postmodern minimalist philosophy, for free over the Internet. Believe it or not! QED! (4/27/09)

The First University for the Masses of the World

The University of Neoliberal Arts is the first university for the masses of the world, and it is free to the masses everywhere in the world through the Internet. I hope that the masses all over the world will take this opportunity to obtain a free world-class education at: http://www.philophysics.com. (4/28/09)

My Explanation of Quantum Mechanics

My explanation of quantum mechanics is as follows: Quantum mechanics is about how probwaves (probability waves) interact with each other in our probwavistic (probability wavistic) brains, in order to give rise to the phenomena that we perceive. In other words, quantum mechanics is about the fundamental aspects of mental phenomena. (4/29/09)

Probwavism Is a Mental Interpretation of What Exists Beyond Appearances

Please note that probwavism (probability wavism) is a mental interpretation of what exists beyond appearances, because human beings can only be aware of their own mental experiences. Therefore, human beings can only conjecture about what exists beyond appearances, if anything, due to the nature of reality. (4/29/09)

The Most Important Concept to Come from My Writings

Personally speaking, the most important concept to come from my writings is the concept that the dead can be resurrected by using panmultiversal panacean computers in order to tap into zero entropy. The people resurrected will be the same people who died, because the mind is eternal, due to the fact that one cannot become more nonexistent than infinite entropy, according to the neolaw of entropy, and infinite entropy is a reversible state of nature. Infinite entropy is a reversible state, because, before we existed, we were infinite entropy states. (4/29/09)

One Cannot Become More Nonexistent
than Infinite Entropy

One cannot become more nonexistent than infinite entropy, according to the neolaw of entropy, and infinite entropy is a reversible state of nature. Therefore, the past is retrievable, because infinite entropy is reversible using panmultiversal panacean computers to tap into zero entropy. (4/29/09)

Creating a World Culture for
the Masses of the World

Neoliberal Arts, aka postmodern minimalist philosophy, is the first serious effort that I know of that is trying to create a world culture for the masses of the world. If I am successful in my goal of making neoliberal Arts the core of a world culture for the masses of the world, the masses of the world would become cultured to an extent that is unsurpassed anywhere in the world today. Believe it or not! QED! (4/29/09)

A Generalist Education Can Be on the Frontiers of Knowledge

I believe that I have succeeded in proving that a generalist (Neoliberal Arts) education can be on the frontiers of knowledge by just consisting of popular media resources, including my writings on my websites. (4/29/09)

One of the Purposes of My Websites

One of the purposes of my websites is to popularize the fact that, contrary to popular and expert opinions, popular media resources are a great source of educational material for the purpose of self-education. I learned this truth by personal experience, which is the best teacher, according to the saying. (4/29/09)

THE MASSES SHOULD
THINK FOR THEMSELVES
(PART FIVE)

Probability Waves Are not Limited by the Speed of Light

Probability waves (probwaves) are not limited by the speed of light, but are instantaneous waves, instead, because they have instantaneous cosmic influence all over the cosmos, and beyond. Probwaves are more evidence why gravity is an instantaneous force. (5/15/09)

The Instantaneity of Probability Waves

The instantaneity of probability waves (probvaves) explains why instantaneous teleportation, and communication to anywhere in the universe and beyond are possible. Please note that the frequencies of the probability waves are unaffected by their instantaneous nature. (5/15/09)

Ethics Is About the Mechanics of Human Social Behavior

Ethics is about the mechanics of human social behavior. In other words, ethical mechanics (ethics) is about the science of social behavior. Ethical mechanics can be mathematized, and it includes morality, social science, social psychology, politics, etc. (5/15/09)

Proof that the Pen Is Mightier than the Sword

In 1972, I proved to the Congress of the United States of America that the pen is mightier than the sword by outlining a plan to remove President Nixon from office, and a plan to defeat the Soviet Union. Both plans were adopted by the Congress, and both plans succeeded. Therefore, I have proved that the pen is mightier than the sword. Proof positive that the pen is mightier than the sword. Believe it or not! QED! (5/15/09)

Ethical Mechanics Is Analogous to Political Mechanics

Ethical mechanics is analogous to political mechanics, and both of them are mathematizable. The Founding Fathers of the USA were ethical and political mechanics of extraordinary quality, because they created a political constitution that was centuries ahead of its time. And, even to this day, the US Constitution has undiscovered ethical and political machanical intricacies that are not fully understood by anyone alive today. And, that is why Americans should be wary about changing their form of government. (5/15/09)

Proof that Duality in Nature Is Inevitable

Proof that duality in nature is inevitable is as follows: The fundamental basis of nature is zero and infinity, which are reciprocals of each other, and therefore inseparable from each other. In other words, nothingness has two fundamental aspects: The zero entropy aspect, and the infinite entropy aspect. Also, all of nature can be divided into abstract and concrete abstractions, which are dualistic in nature. Therefore, everything in nature is dualistic, because everything in nature is the characteristics of zero or nothingness, which has two fundamental co-equal aspects: zero and infinity; or zero entropy and infinite entropy. Therefore, I have proven that duality is inevitable. Proof positive that duality in nature is inevitable. Believe it or not! QED! (5/16/09)

Religious People and Free Will

Religious people believe in free will, so that they can celebrate and believe in the coming dictatorship of God, where it will be a sin to exercise free will. In other words, religious people long to become God's robots. (5/16/09)

Religious People Long to Become God's Robots

Religious people long to become God's robots, because they do not really believe in free will, but they think a lot about free will, so that they can celebrate and believe in the coming dictatorship of God, where it will be a sin to exercise free will. (5/16/09)

The Mind and the Soul

The mind is the nonzero aspect of the self, while the soul is the zero aspect of the self. The nonzero aspect of the self can never perceive the the zero aspect of the self directly, and that is why human beings can never know God directly, because a person's soul is their personal God, and the nonzero aspect of the self can never achieve zero entropy, which is the state in which the soul exists at all times. However, the self can achieve infinite entropy when we are unconscious, because the unconscious state is the infinite entropy state. (5/17/09)

Resurrection and Panmultiversal Panacean Computers

No religious texts explain how God will resurrect the dead, so human beings are free to speculate on such matters. I believe that God will use human beings to resurrect the dead by means of panmultiversal panacean computers (PPCs), because God helps those who help themselves, as the saying goes. Folks, PPCs are looking more and more likely as time goes by, because of the great advances that are being made in quantum entanglement computer research (QECR). (5/17/09)

Human Beings Are Free to Speculate About Spiritual Technology

Human beings are free to speculate about spiritual technology, because no religious texts disallow such speculation, and God helps those who help themselves, as the saying goes. So, human beings should feel free to speculate about how spiritual technology works, because spiritual phenomena can only be accomplished with spiritual technology. Believe it or not! QED! (5/17/09)

The Ferreira Genesis Equation and Infinite Regresses

The Ferreira Genesis Equation does not rule out infinite regresses, because the Ferreira Genesis Equation rules out nothing. In fact, there can even be an infinite regress of Ferreira Genesis Equations. So, the question: Who created God? is not an absurd question, because the question of who created God involves an infinite regress, and infinite regresses are not ruled out by the Ferreira Genesis Equation, due to the fact that infinite regresses are mathematically consistent. (5/17/09)

Panaceanism and World Politics

Panaceanism will be taking on a larger and larger role in world politics, because panaceanism is about panmultiversal panacean computers (PPCs), which are the ultimate technology. The elites of the world are already scrambling to determine how they are going to exploit and control PPCs. In other words, PPCs are already reshaping the international politics of the future. So far, it does not look so good for the masses of the world, but things can change in favor of the masses, if the masses of the world were to study my websites, now. Believe it or not! QED! (5/17/09)

Infinite Regresses Are Mathematically Consistent

Infinite regresses are mathematically consistent. Therefore, infinite regresses can not be ruled out in nature, because nature is mathematical, due to the Ferreira Fundamental Trinity, which consists of concrete and abstract language, logic, and mathematics. (5/18/09)

Blowing the Whistle on the Clergy

Do the masses ever wonder why the clergy all over the world tell their flocks that philosophy is crap, when philosophy is a mandatory subject in all religious seminaries all over the world? The answer is simple: the clergy wants to keep the masses ignorant, so that the clergy can exploit their flocks at will. (5/18/09)

Philosophy Makes Science and Religion Strange Bedfellows

Do the masses ever wonder why philosophy makes science and religion strange bedfellows? The answer is simple: Philosophy is the key to educating the masses, and scientists and the clergy want to keep the masses ignorant, so that science and religion can exploit the masses. What the masses do not know is that scientists and the clergy are closet philosophers, who do not want the masses to be educated in philosophy, because knowledge is power, and the elites of the world do not want the masses to gain power through education in philosophy. (5/18/09)

Religion and Science Believe in Thought Police

Religion and science believe in thought police for different reasons. Religion believes in thought police for religious reasons, while science believes in thought police for scientific reasons. Both religion and science would like to silence each other, and they would both like to silence philosophy, because philosophy is the key to educating the masses. (5/18/09)

The Ferreira Genesis Equation Rules out Nothing

The Ferreira Genesis Equation rules out nothing, because the Ferreira Genesis Equation encompasses everything that is possible in nature. In other words, the Ferreira Genesis Equation states that anything is possible in nature. (5/19/09)

There Are no Ideas in Philosophy that the Masses Cannot Understand

Philosophy is the key to educating the masses, because philosophy is understandable by the masses, if philosophy is simplified for the masses. There are no ideas in philosophy that the masses cannot understand, if the philosophical ideas are simplified for the masses. Philosophy is the most profound and enlightening form of knowledge known to human beings, and it just so happens that the masses can comprehend philosophy. The masses should wonder why the elites of society do not want them to study philosophy, if the elites of society really cared about the masses. (5/19/09)

Most of the Elites of Society Are Closet Philosophers

The masses should wonder why most of the elites of society are closet philosophers, when the public posture of most of the elites of society is that philosophy is crap? The answer is that philosophy is the food of the Gods, and most of the elites of society do not want to share the food of the Gods with the masses, and that is why most of the elites of society hold this hypocritical view of philosophy in public. I want the masses to trust me when I say that philosophy is not crap, because I want the masses to be educated like me. (5/20/09)

Proof that Non-Western Countries Can Leapfrog the West

Neoliberal Arts is proof positive that non-Western countries can leapfrog the West, because I was born on a small island in the Caribbean, and Neoliberal Arts is my creation. And, I can assure non-Western countries that Neoliberal Arts has already leapfrogged the West, intellectually speaking. Believe it or not! QED! (5/20/09)

The Soul of the Self Is God

The soul of the self is God, because the soul of the self has zero entropy, and zero entropy is God, according to the neolaw of entropy, while the mind of the self is the self, because the mind of the self has nonzero entropy, and nonzero entropy is the mind of the self, according to the neolaw of entropy. Since solipsism is true from each person's perspective, it means that the soul of the self is God from the perspective of the self. (5/20/09)

Proof that Each Creative C Student Is Worth Ten Thousand Noncreative A Students

Neoliberal Arts is proof positive that each creative C student is worth about ten thousand noncreative A students, because I was a creative C student in school, and Neoliberal Arts is my creation. And, I can assure the world that it would have taken about ten thousand former noncreative A students to create Neoliberal Arts. Therefore, countries that do not make full use of their creative C students now will have the rest of eternity to regret it. Believe it or not! QED! (5/22/09)

Why Does God Tolerate Evil in the World?

God tolerates evil in the world, because God's actions in creation are governed by the neolaw of entropy, which is about the struggle between entropy and anti-entropy for the dominance of nature. In other words, the neolaw of entropy governs our souls, which are our subconscious minds from our individual perspectives. Not forgetting, of course, that solipsism is true from our individual perspectives, because all that we perceive are the characteristics of our own minds, and physical existence is an unproven, and an unprovable hypothesis. Therefore, we can never detect the existence of other minds than our own. Believe it or not! QED! (5/22/09)

Fluvirologism

Fluvirologism is the philosophical doctrine that states that there are basically three types of flu viruses: The first type is the biological influenza (influencer) viruses; the second type is the computer software influencer (influenza) viruses; and the third type is the human ideational influencer (influenza) viruses. All three types of flu viruses have many characteristics in common that can be studied scientifically. In fact, governments around the world release different types of flu viruses into the environment in order to study the spread and control of all three types of flu viruses. It should be noted that human ideational influencer (influenza) viruses can either be entropic or anti-entropic in nature. (5/22/09)

Original Ideas Are Analogous to Prime Numbers

Original ideas are analogous to prime numbers, which are inexhaustible even for panmultiversal panacean computers, because there is an infinite number of prime numbers. Therefore, philosophers should celebrate this fact, because it means that they have the rest of eternity to discover new original ideas. (5/23/09)

All the Fundamental Laws of
Nature Might Be Statistical

All the fundamental laws of nature might be statistical, because if all the fundamental laws of nature are statistical, it would explain why statistics is so unusually effective at quantifying nature. Personally speaking, I believe that all the fundamental laws of nature are statistical, because statistics is a good use of Occam's razor, especially in quantum mechanics. (5/24/09)

Eugenics Is Obsolete

Eugenics is obsolete, because panmultiversal panacean computers (PPCs) will be able to transform all human beings into the eMessiahs, which are the beings that the alchemists of old were trying to create with their alchemy. (5/24/09)

The Federal Reserve System Is Unconstitutional

The Federal Reserve System (The Fed) is unconstitutional, because it is unaccountable to the US Congress, which are the representatives of the people of the United States of America under the US Constitution. I am surprised that the Congress has allowed the Fed to exist in its current form for so long. (5/24/09)

The Uniform Code of Military Justice Is not Above the US Constitution

The Uniform Code of Military Justice (UCMJ) is not above the US Constitution, because nothing is above the US Constitution for US nationals anywhere in the world. So, all talk that military personnel give up all their Constitutional rights when they join the US Military is crap, because the US Constitution is the supreme law of the land of the USA. (5/24/09)

In Philosophy, the Citing of
Sources Can Prove Nothing

In philosophy, the citing of sources is a scam, because the citing of sources can prove nothing. Philosophical ideas should stand or fall on their own merits, because the citing of sources adds nothing to the truth or falsity of philosophical ideas. (5/24/09)

Neoliberal Arts Is a Form of Postmodern
Minimalist Literature

Neoliberal Arts is a form of postmodern minimalist literature (PML), because it is a bridge discipline that links, interprets, and critiques all branches of learning using the aphorism and the short article. In other words, postmoderm minimalist literature (PML) is mostly nonfictional, but it can also be fictional. Also, postmodern minimalist literature (PML) is the most concise, simple, clear, and profound form of literature in the world. (5/25/09)

Nothing Exists Outside of the Mind

From the perspective of the mind, nothing exists outside of the mind, because all that the mind perceives is the characteristics of the mind, and physical existence is an unproven and an unprovable hypothesis. Therefore, the mind has primacy over fundamental particles, because fundamental particles are mental phenomena. (5/26/09)

Fundamental Particles Are Mental Phenomena

Fundamental particles are mental phenomena, because all that we perceive are the characteristics of our own minds, and physical existence is an unproven and an unprovable hypothesis. Therefore, the mind has primacy over fundamental particles, because fundamental particles are mental phenomena. (5/26/09)

The Mind Appears to Be Vast, Because It Is Vast

The mind appears to be vast, because it is vast, due to the fact that the mind encompasses everything in creation from the perspective of the self. In other words, the mind is not confined to the interior of the brain, because the brain is only one aspect of the mind, although the brain is vital for consciousness to occur. (5/26/09)

No Mind Can Be Said to Exist Inside or Outside of Another Mind

It should be noted that, if other minds exist other than our own, they cannot be said to exist inside or outside of our minds, but, in fact, they would exist in other realities, which cannot be said to exist inside or outside of our minds, because no mind can be said to exist inside or outside of another mind, according to solipsism. (5/26/09)

Adverse Stimulation and Human Creativity

Adverse (entropic) stimulation causes the human brain to greater levels of creativity than it would normally be capable of, because adverse stimulation is more useful than nonadverse stimulation for the creative output of human beings. (5/27/09)

The American Eagle

Politically speaking, the American Eagle represents anything from the dove of peace to the hawk of war, because the American Eagle has in one claw an olive branch, and in the other claw a quiver of arrows. (5/27/09)

Self-Hate and Self-Love

Entropy is about self-hate, while anti-entropy is about self-love, because all that we perceive are the characteristics of our own minds, and physical existence is an unproven, and an unprovable hypothesis. (5/28/09)

Education and Influencer (Influenza) Viruses

Education is about infecting students with human ideational influencer (influenza) viruses, which can either be entropic or anti-entropic in nature depending on the desired results that the educators are trying to achieve. (5/28/09)

There Is an Infinite Number of Ferreira Genesis Equations

There is an infinite number of Ferreira Genesis Equations (FGEs), because each mind is a separate Ferreira Genesis Equation (FGE), and there is an infinite number of potential minds that exist in nature as infinite entropy states. It should be noted that all FGEs are interrelated, although they exist as separate realities. (5/28/09)

Trial and Error and the Philosophical Enterprise

Philosophers are making a big mistake by trying to eliminate trial and error from the philosophical enterprise, because original ideas are analogous to prime numbers, and prime numbers are situated at random within the integer number line. Besides that, trial and error is still an important part of science, so it is idiotic to try to eliminate trial and error from philosophy. Believe it or not! QED! (5/28/09)

Proof that Most Geniuses Cannot Make It All the Way Through Academia

I am proof positive that most geniuses cannot make it all the way through academia, because I am an average genius, and the furthest that I got in my formal education is two years of college. Before I entered college, I told Congress that I was going to fail in my pursuit of a college education, and I did. I hope that everyone can see that I am a genius, because all my ideas are on my websites, including those which I gave to the US Government in 1972. Thus, I have proven my point. Believe it or not! QED! (5/28/09)

Unlocking the Secrets of Nothing

I believe that I have unlocked the secrets of nothing with my Ferreira Genesis Equation (FGE), because the FGE has unlocked a cornucopia of ideas dealing with the nature of nothing. I predict that the nature of nothing will become major fields of scientific and philosophical study in the future, because the nature of nothing is the key to understanding everything. (5/28/09)

The Fallacy that Something Cannot Come from Nothing

It is a fallacy that something cannot come from nothing, because everything consists of the characteristics of nothing. And, besides that, nothing is a state that consists of two fundamental states: the zero entropy state, and the infinite entropy state. In other words, nothing is really something. Therefore, something can come from nothing, according to the Ferreira Genesis Equation. (5/29/09)

The Neolaw of Entropy Is to Blame for the State of the World

The neolaw of entropy is to blame for the state of the world, because human beings are creatures of the neolaw of entropy. The neolaw of entropy states that existence is a struggle between entropy and anti-entropy for the dominance of nature. In other words, the human mind is a battle ground between entropy and anti-entropy for the dominance of the self. (5/29/09)

The Human Mind Is a Battle Ground Between Entropy and Anti-Entropy

The human mind is a battle ground between entropy and anti-entropy for the dominance of the self, because all that we perceive are the characteristics of our own minds, and physical existence is an unproven, and an unprovable hypothesis. In other words, the neolaw of entropy is to blame for the state of our minds. (5/29/09)

The Neolaw of Entropy Is to Blame for the State of Our Minds

The neolaw of entropy is to blame for the state of our minds at all times, because the neolaw of entropy governs everything in nature, including God. The neolaw of entropy is still a hypothesis, because it hasn't been mathematized and verified as yet, but I am pretty certain that it is correct. (5/29/09)

Everyone Is Much Wealthier than They Think

Everyone is much wealthier than they think, because everything that they perceive is the characteristics of their own minds, and physical existence is an unproven, and an unprovable hypothesis. Therefore, the only reason why each individual cannot exercise sovereignty over everything that they perceive is because of the neolaw of entropy, which states that existence is about the struggle between entropy and anti-entropy for the dominance of nature. (5/29/09)

INDEX